MINDSET FIRST MONEY SECOND

THE THINGS I DID TO STOP LIVING PAYCHECK TO PAYCHECK...FOR GOOD

JB MCGINNIS

with Mel Brown McGinnis

POWERED
PUBLISHING

ISBN: 979-8-9884458-0-7

Published by
MPowered Sports and Entertainment, LLC
dba MPowered Publishing
Cedar Hill, Texas

Printed in the United States of America

All text and works of literature featured in *Mindset First Money Second: The Things I Did to Stop Living Paycheck to Paycheck... for Good* are the original intellectual properties of Jeffrey B. McGinnis and Mel Brown McGinnis (collectively "author") unless otherwise noted.

Contributing Author: Mel Brown McGinnis
Cover Design: Daniel Ojedokun
Back Cover Photo: Sandra Hill

DEDICATION

To my dear wife, I dedicate this book to you with love and gratitude. Your unwavering support, encouragement, and patience have been essential in bringing this project to fruition. You were with me every step of the way, helping me construct and refine my ideas, reading and editing my drafts, and offering valuable insight and feedback. Without you, this book would not exist. You are not only my wife but also my best friend and partner. I am blessed to have you in my life, and I thank you for everything you do for me.

To my beloved daughter, raising you has been the greatest achievement of my life. Watching you grow into a strong, loving, and compassionate woman has filled me with pride and joy. You have taught me the meaning of unconditional love. You have inspired me to be a better man, and I hope I have made you proud. I dedicate this book to you with all my love, and I pray it inspires you to pursue your dreams with courage and passion.

ACKNOWLEDGMENTS

This book is the product of a lifetime of experiences, reflections, and conversations. It is a testament to the power of discipline, family, and love, and it would not be possible without the support of those closest to me. Thank you, all, for your continuous support, insightful feedback, and unwavering love.

To my mom, Sandra, and my Aunt Debra, who established the foundation of my life; to my dad, who taught me many of life's invaluable lessons; to my brothers and sisters for being my sounding boards throughout my life; to my aunts and uncles who instilled the love of family and legacy within me; and to my entire family and my wife's family, thank you for always supporting us in everything we do.

Much love to my Deneen and Dunbar families, Army battle buddies, Masonic Brothers, and Quiznos and Carrington families.

Special thanks to my readers Ruby McGinnis, Gary Daniels, and Michael Brundy.

To all of my fraternity brothers of Kappa Alpha Psi Fraternity Inc., especially the Arlington-Grand Prairie Alumni Chapter (TX), and the Mighty Southwestern Province, I say Yo!

MESSAGE TO THE READER

The most important thing you need to know about this book is that I'm not trying to make you a millionaire...not today, anyway. Eventually, you could achieve millionaire status if you follow this plan, but if you're looking to "get rich quick," this book is NOT for you. My goal with this book is to give you practical tips and guidelines to help you become financially independent and sustain it for life. I developed the "1/3 Financial System" to provide a simple way for the average person to learn healthy money habits and understand how to start building a financial legacy. It allowed me to retire at the age of 44 and establish my financial legacy to provide for my family's future.

If you're struggling financially, this book will help you get started on the path to financial freedom.

If you're doing okay financially, this book will provide you with financial guidance and a proven process to become even more financially successful.

If you're doing well financially, *Mindset First Money Second: The Things I Did to Stop Living Paycheck to Paycheck... for Good* may help you become financially independent. By financially independent, I mean having residual income to take care of your monthly expenses without working.

Because I wrote this book, you don't have to go through the hard stuff to try and figure it out. I've done the work.

I've done the research. I've personally dealt with every concept in this book that I'm going to tell you about. I've already made the mistakes, so you don't have to. I've spent two decades learning and perfecting these lessons. It's up to you to utilize the methods I've perfected so that you, too, can become financially independent. Financial independence is great, but I never said it would be easy. You will have to do the work and sacrifice some things that might make you uncomfortable. But if you want to be financially independent, and you have the desire to do what it takes, then this book is for you. If you have read this message to this point, then you're halfway there!

This system works. It has worked for me. It has worked for others. It can work for you. Follow the plan and stay financially healthy. Keeping your finances in order is a lifetime commitment, so you have to stay updated. The best part about the lessons in this book is that you can tailor the plan to fit your life.

What I need from you...

Be honest with yourself about your money situation;
Don't give up...it's going to be challenging;
Step outside of your box to achieve success;
Evaluate your progress, and adjust fire as needed.

NOW LET'S GET STARTED!

MINDSET FIRST
MONEY SECOND

THE THINGS I DID TO STOP LIVING PAYCHECK TO PAYCHECK...FOR GOOD.

TABLE OF CONTENTS

"

This book will give you first-hand
insight on the things I did to stop
living paycheck to paycheck.

"

INTRODUCTION

In order to change your financial mindset and develop healthy financial habits, you must have systems for your life. For example, you should have a system or a process that you consistently implement for buying cars, shopping for groceries, maintaining your health, buying homes, setting your budget, etc. Doing things in a consistent manner over a consistent period of time is critical. As we go through the material, we will work on developing systems for each of the concepts covered in this book. A few things I'm really excited to share with you are what I call *"Mindset Matters."* These are twenty-five quick tips that have nothing to do with money, but have everything to do with money, and they will help you achieve long-term financial success.

I'm certainly not saying that my way is the only way, but I am saying these systems have worked for me throughout my life. The greatest thing about the concepts in this book is that they can be modified to fit YOUR lifestyle and YOUR circumstances so you can develop YOUR own systems that will work for you.

This book will give you first-hand insight on the things I did to stop living paycheck to paycheck.

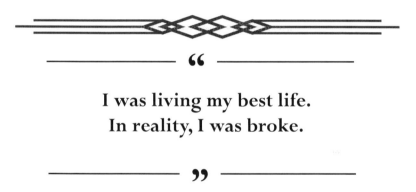

I was living my best life.
In reality, I was broke.

Jbm Seminars

The National Bureau of Economic Research reveals that individuals with low levels of financial literacy are more likely to engage in costly financial behaviors, such as carrying high-interest debt or making poor investment decisions.[1]

---

1. Annamaria Lusardi and Olivia Mitchell. "The Outlook for Financial Literacy," National Bureau of Economic Research, May 2011. https://www. nber.org/papers/w17077.

I.
FIRST THINGS FIRST …
FIND YOUR EPIPHANY

Have you ever heard the expression, "You won't change until you hit rock bottom?" There's a lot of truth to that. I didn't truly realize what rock bottom was, until I hit it. My problem was when I thought I was at my lowest point and I couldn't get any lower, I didn't do anything about it.

I was a soldier in Wonju, South Korea, and you would think I was living my best life. In reality, I was broke. I ignored the signs that my financial rock bottom was near. So of course, things kept getting worse and worse and worse and worse.

But I still wasn't at rock bottom.

I thought I was at rock bottom when the bill collectors were calling me every day trying to collect payments on my three maxed out credit cards and my car payment.

I wasn't there yet.

I thought I was at rock bottom when the constant late payments plummeted my credit score from the 500s to somewhere in the neighborhood of the 400s.

I wasn't there yet.

Nope. Not yet. How do I know? Because I kept spending money like I didn't owe it to anyone.

One of the things I loved about being in Korea was that you could get a tailor-made suit for $100 in three days, so why would I not have seven of them? Impulse shopping at its finest. There were so many options: designer leather coats, Gucci, Louis Vuitton, whatever latest fashion trend you could think of, and indistinguishable knock-offs at your fingertips. Korea was a shopper's paradise, and I was spending money left and right! I was the kid who majored in tailoring at Dunbar Vocational High School on the southside of Chicago, so being in Korea, I felt like a kid in a candy store. If you could think of it, they could make it.

I once saw Babyface in a magazine, and he had on a sharp suit. I ripped out the page from the magazine and took it to Mr. Kim (I may not have his name correct, but my point is there was a tailor on every corner).

I asked Mr. Kim, "Can you make this for me?"

He said, "Come back in three days. I will have it for you."

Korea, 1990: I was as broke as a joke...
but I looked good!

It was too easy. The only problem was that every month, I found myself flat broke two weeks after every payday with little to no money in my pocket, or my bank account. The calls, the threats, not being able to pay my bills and living paycheck to paycheck weighed heavily on me, and it was embarrassing. Yet, I kept doing the same things I had been doing. Then, one day, the phone rang.

If you think bill collectors won't find you anywhere in the world, think again! I was in the barracks on a military installation on the side of a mountain in Wonju, South Korea, and my phone rang. Korean phone numbers had eighteen characters, and the only people who had that phone number were my mother and my sister back home in Chicago. There was no caller ID on phones at that time, but I answered the phone because I thought something might be wrong back home.

"Hello?"

A male voice comes on the line. "Hi, is this Mr. McGinnis?"

"Yes, this is SGT. McGinnis. Who is this?"

"This is John with Ford Financial. I'm calling about the payments on your Mustang. You're four months behind on your payments. If you can't make the payments, we can take that car off your hands and just call it good."

I asked myself, "How in the hell did he find me in freaking Korea?"

John said, "We can pick it up as soon as tomorrow."

I was devastated. This was just too much. They were trying to take away my pride and joy... Ghost... my diamond white Mustang GT 5.0 with five-star rims on one side, Euro mesh on the other, and personalized license plates that phonetically read "HY-OFISR."

This was too much. I talked to John about payment arrangements that would get me caught up and allow me to keep my car. I couldn't let my car get repossessed. That was something that happened to other people, not me. I knew in that moment that I had to get my life together. That was my epiphany. Before that phone rang though, I was walking around Korea like I owned it. After that phone call with John, I knew it was time to do something different. I was about to get custody of my nine-year-old daughter when I got back to the States, and I was at rock bottom. I knew I had to do better, if not for me, then for her.

MINDSET CHECK √

Have you had your epiphany? If so, what was it?

What are your **top three takeaways** from this chapter?

How will you change or maintain your mindset to achieve financial success?

_____

_____

_____

_____

_____

_____

_____

_____

_____

_____

_____

_____

_____

_____

_____

_____

_____

_____

_____

_____

_____

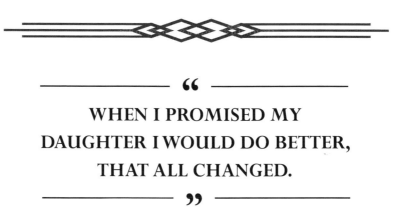

WHEN I PROMISED MY DAUGHTER I WOULD DO BETTER, THAT ALL CHANGED.

Jbm Seminars

According to a 2021 study by the Federal Reserve, 32% of Americans surveyed cannot cover an unexpected $400 expense without borrowing money or selling something.[2]

2. "Economic Well-being of U.S. Households (SHED)," Board of Governors of the Federal Reserve System, May 2022. https://www.federalreserve.gov/publications/2022-economic-well-being-of-us-households-in-2021-dealing-with-unexpected-expenses.htm.

II.

PROMISE SOMEONE ELSE
BESIDES YOURSELF

I have promised myself many, many times that I would do better with something and then failed to get it done. Whether it was eating right, being more disciplined, improving my finances, it didn't matter. The problem I had when I failed myself was there was no accountability; no real consequences or repercussions. When I promised my daughter I would do better, that all changed.

My daughter and I in 1995.

I have always been in my daughter's life, but I got full custody of her when she was nine-years-old. When she came from Chicago to Fort Stewart, Georgia, to live with me, I remember going to the airport to pick her up. At that time, there was no TSA, and you could walk up to the terminal and watch your loved ones come down the jet way.

My mom, my sister, and two of my nephews came along with her. I thought back to being a young man and helping my mom take care of my baby sister who was thirteen years younger than me. This would be different. This was a little human who depended on me for a successful life, and I was scared. Actually, I was terrified I might not get it right.

Then I saw my daughter get off the plane. She had all of her worldly possessions in a small shoulder bag, she was wearing an outfit that I knew I would never let her wear again, and the look on her face said everything I needed to know.

She looked up at me, and I could see in her eyes that she was saying *"Hey, dude, I hope you have your sh*t together because I really need you."* My daughter had a pretty rough upbringing to that point, but I realized at that moment I had to do better because she needed me. She needed a stable home, she needed real friends, and she needed predictability and peace.

Seeing her like that scared me. I was nervous. I had been a single guy all my life and now I had this little person to take care of who was depending on me for security and a good home. That's when I looked at her and said, "Daughter, I got you."

Before I brought her home, I made sure her room was all set up. She had a brass bed that I purchased while stationed in Korea, a big TV, a VCR, and a desk, all the things a growing pre-teen girl would need. She never had anything like that before in her life.

She looked at me and asked with excitement, "Is all of this mine?"

"Yes, daughter," I said.

That moment, I promised my daughter that she would never have to struggle like I did. She wouldn't have to worry about having food to eat. She wouldn't have to worry about having a roof over her head. She wouldn't have to be concerned about her school trips getting canceled because an unexpected bill came up. I promised her I would do better. That solidified it for me. I never wanted to see disappointment in her face because of a bad decision I made.

That took me over the edge, that was it for me. That's when I turned the corner. My daughter made me a more responsible man. My daughter was *my* accountability.

Now let's talk about *you*. If you have failed at succeeding on your own, promise someone you love that you won't fail. If you don't want to look in their eyes and see the disappointment, promise them that you will become financially stable. Promise them that you will get your financial house in order. Is that person your child, your mom, your brother, your sister, your spouse? Whoever it is, use that person as motivation to help you take the next step. Sometimes we have to feel accountable to someone besides ourselves to get something done.

For example, if you promise your best friend you will do something, you will probably get it done, no matter what you have to do to complete the task. But if you promise yourself, you may be more likely to put it off until another day. Find that person that will hold you accountable and that you can be accountable to. Promise them that you will succeed, and do whatever you need to do to keep that promise.

MINDSET CHECK √

Who is that person that gives you external motivation to succeed?

What are your **top three takeaways** from this chapter?

How will you change or maintain your mindset to achieve financial success?

_____

_____

_____

_____

_____

_____

_____

_____

_____

_____

_____

_____

_____

_____

_____

_____

_____

_____

_____

_____

> "Generally, no one comes to you when you're five-years-old and says 'this is how you manage money.'

Jbm Seminars

A January 2023 research series performed by LendingClub Corporation (NYSE: LC), the parent company of America's leading digital marketplace bank, found that 60% of Americans live paycheck to paycheck, down four percentage points from January 2022.[3]

3. "Today's Paycheck to Paycheck Landscape," Lending Club Corporation, February 28, 2023. https://ir.lendingclub.com/news/news-details/2023/60-of-Americans-Now-Living-Paycheck-to-Paycheck-Down-from-64-a-Month-Ago/default.aspx.

III.

PSYCHOLOGICAL ASPECTS
OF DEBT

The cycle of living paycheck to paycheck often starts early. Most people learn how to manage money from watching the people around them as they grow up. Generally, no one comes to you when you're five-years-old and says, "This is how you manage money." Often times, you learn before you're actually taught.

I grew up in a poor Chicago neighborhood in a 14-story high rise on the southside that we affectionately called "The White Building." I learned how to manage money watching my mom, who probably wasn't the best example.

The *cycle* went something like this: Mom gets paid; Mom goes to the grocery store; Mom buys groceries; Mom gets caught up on bills; Mom is broke within three days of getting paid; we eat beans and hot water cornbread for the next week and a half; Mom gets paid again; repeat.

If Mom had any extra money, she would spend her money on whatever. Never saved it, always spend it. One week it could be Garrett Popcorn, the next time it could be a special type of fudge from downtown.

The fudge was expensive, but it tasted so good! I grew up with three siblings (my baby sister came later), and if Mom bought fudge, she would break a small piece for each of us. That was our special thing. The fudge.

I watched my mother handle money like this for years. This was the spending style I adopted as a kid and during my early adult years. I thought this was normal, good or bad. I thought this was the way you were supposed to manage money. It was normal—get paid, buy food, pay your bills, buy you something special, and do it all over again.

When I went into the Army, I had more money than I ever had in my life. After groceries and bills, I found special things to spend money on just like Mom. Whether I spent money on clothes, rims for my car, gold chains, etc, I just thought it was normal to spend all of my money.

Eventually, I realized this was not getting me anywhere because I was stuck in this cycle where I never had any money left and struggled with life until the next paycheck.

My cycle (just like my mom's) went something like this: get paid; go to the grocery store; buy groceries; pay bills; spend extra money on whatever; three days before the next payday eat ramen and Vienna sausage; get paid again; repeat.

It wasn't until I identified my psychological aspects of debt that I was able to break the cycle of living paycheck to paycheck.

Four Main Psychological Aspects of Debt

- Impulse Buying
- Last Minute Buying
- Self-Esteem Buying
- Ostrich Effect

IMPULSE BUYING

What is it?

Buying items on a whim without much thought or consideration.

Why do we do it?

Convenience.

At some point, we all fall victim to impulse buying. You might be checking out in the grocery store and need that pack of peanut M&Ms because you're craving sugar; or all of a sudden, you're parched and "need" a pop or a soda; or at this very moment your curiosity is peaked and that magazine featuring Drake and Rihanna is a must read.

These things are placed on the shelves on your way out of the grocery store for a reason. Businesses hope you will be impulsive on your way out and buy certain items on a whim without much thought or consideration to how much you're spending or if you really "need" those items. This is exactly why every grocery store has things at the cash register. These items are often low in cost and generally won't have any real impact on your budget. Many shoppers see them as minor purchases.

But what about the big-ticket items that you buy on a whim? For example, Johnny goes to Best Buy to buy a TV. His friend Tom tags along for support. Johnny buys a 75" TV to put in his new apartment. Tom, who already has two TVs in his apartment, decides to buy the same TV because the sale is so great he can't pass it up. Tom doesn't need another TV, but because the TV was on sale,

Tom buys one too. Tom totally bought the TV on impulse simply because of the sale.

Here's What Worked for Me ...

There are many tactics you can use to manage (not avoid because we're all human) impulse buying:

- Identify what impulse buying actually is and is not;
- Purchase needs vs. wants;
- Take a list to the store, and only buy what's on the list (make sure your list is complete before you leave, i.e., if you're cooking from a recipe, make sure all of the ingredients you need are on the list).

LAST-MINUTE BUYING

What is it?
Purchasing items at the last minute when you're under extreme pressure. The item becomes critical, and you probably could have paid less if you bought the item in advance.

Why do we do it?
Procrastination.

This is the age-old issue of waiting until the last minute to buy things. It gets hot and intense with the timeline and you end up making a purchase that likely costs you more at the time of purchase than it would have had you purchased in advance.

Example #1 – How many times have you put off buying an airline ticket for so long the ticket significantly increased in price? Purchasing the ticket becomes a last-minute buy because your trip is in two weeks.

Example #2 – You know you need new tires, but you wait and wait and wait, and then you have a blow out on the freeway! Now you're on the side of the road with a blown-out tire, and not only do you have to spend money to replace the tire, you also have to spend money to get your vehicle towed. Now it's a last-minute buy because your transportation is in jeopardy.

Example #3 – You hear a knocking sound in your car, knowing you need a repair, but you're busy so you never take your vehicle to the shop. It could be your brakes or muffler, who knows what it is, but it inevitably ends up costing you more now that the problem is really bad. You waited until the issue was critical, and now it's a last-minute buy because it's crucial to get it fixed or you won't have transportation.

According to Dr. Itamar Shatz, PhD, author of the recent article, "Why People Procrastinate: The Psychology and Causes of Procrastination," a few of the most common hindering factors as to why people procrastinate are:[4]

Tasks that are far in the future (i.e., "I have time")
Anxiety
Feeling overwhelmed
Fear of failure
Depression

---

4. Dr. Itamar Shatz, PhD. "Why People Procrastinate: The Psychology and Causes of Procrastination," Solving Procrastination. Accessed September 2, 2023. https://solving procrastination.com/why-people-procrastinate/.

Avoid procrastination – Procrastination often leads to last minute spending. Generally, items are more expensive when you procrastinate and end up costing two to four times the amount you normally would have paid had you bought the item ahead of time.

Reminders – Set reminders on your phone or on your calendar. Complete the task immediately when the reminder comes up.

Deadlines – Give yourself deadlines to get things done. Make a list and check items off as you complete them.

SELF-ESTEEM BUYING

What is it?
Buying items that make you feel accomplished, accepted, or a part of the "in-crowd."

Why do we do it?
Popularity, pride, peer pressure, notoriety, flexing, to be a part of the "cool clique," or we want to be known as having a high income.

There is absolutely nothing wrong with buying name brand items. Sometimes the higher the value and the bigger the name brand, the better the quality item. However, when you're trying to develop healthy spending habits, and learn not to live paycheck to paycheck, whether something is a name brand shouldn't be the determining factor in whether you buy it. There are some people who will not shop at discount stores. They must have name brand items (Gucci, Louis Vuitton, Prada, Nike, etc). Sometimes, people are concerned with how they will be viewed by others and will not buy certain items unless the item is a name brand. This is what can keep you in trouble.

As I was raising my daughter, when the latest fashion craze came out, I would try to buy that item on sale or shop when the item was out of season. If you shop for long sleeve items in the summer, the price is generally lower, and you can often get the name brand item on sale in the off-season. During the winter, buy shorts and short sleeve shirts.

Holidays – The day after Halloween and Christmas, you can often get everything 50%-60% off, especially costumes, decorations, and novelty items. Only buying name brand items, especially when they don't align with your budget, can be crippling to developing healthy financial habits and crippling to your budget.

Here's What Worked for Me ...

- Buy on sale;
- Buying out of season;
- Shop at stores you wouldn't think carry those items because they are usually lower priced;
- Shop at outlet malls, thrift stores, and smaller department stores. You might be surprised at what you find.

OSTRICH EFFECT:

What is it?

There is a common saying that "an ostrich sticks its head in the sand when it perceives danger." This isn't necessarily true, but the ostrich effect from a financial perspective is avoiding situations when you may receive unpleasant information related to finances.

Example - If a bill collector calls, you ignore the call. If a past due bill comes in the mail, you don't open it.

Why do we do it?
To avoid uncomfortable situations or circumstances, and the reality that you are up to your neck in debt.

The quickest way to address the ostrich effect is to attack it head on. In order to have your financial house in order, you have to be responsible enough to face the issues and come up with a plan to resolve the problem. If you find yourself or someone you know in this situation, sit down, open up the bills, determine how much you owe, and come up with a budget to pay off the debt. If you haven't already done so, get a copy of your credit report from each of the reporting agencies[5] and compare what the bill collector reported to the credit bureaus with the bills you received.

What should you do?

Call the bill collectors directly:

– Set up a payment plan;
– Negotiate a reduction in the monthly amount due;

---

5. Everyone is entitled to one free report each year from all three of the credit reporting agencies. Ordering these once a year will not harm your credit score. You can get these at www.annualcreditreport.com.

- Negotiate a reduction in the APR (annual percentage rate) which reduces the total amount owed; or
- Negotiate a reduction in the balance (this is generally considered a settlement and should be a last resort because typically this will be reported to the credit agencies as a charge-off and remain on your credit report longer).

Things to avoid:

Unless you have disposable income, one thing I suggest you avoid is going to a "credit repair company" or "fixer." Fixing your credit is something you can do yourself if you're willing to put in the time. Now, if you can afford to pay a "fixer," and you know you're not going to do it yourself, then by all means, hire a fixer. However, chances are if you can't afford to pay your bills, you likely can't afford to pay a "fixer." The best thing to do is to gather all of your past due notices, pull your credit reports, and come up with a plan of action to get your debt paid off. There are some non-profit organizations that will assist you if you would like to explore that option.

Remember, when you're on the road to success, you have to be diligent and aware of pitfalls to avoid falling back into old habits. Make sure you have some cheerleaders in your corner and give yourself reminders that you are shooting for a better life.

Remember your *why* in getting your mindset right when it comes to making healthy financial decisions. Make sure you keep that in your back pocket if things get tough.

MINDSET CHECK √

What are your **top three takeaways** from this chapter?

How will you change or maintain your mindset to achieve financial success?

_____

_____

_____

_____

_____

_____

_____

_____

_____

_____

_____

_____

_____

_____

_____

_____

_____

_____

_____

_____

"

The key to success with having
money is to get comfortable with
not spending it as soon as you
get it.

"

Jbm Seminars

According to a recent poll conducted by CNBC and Momentive, at least 53% of Americans surveyed admit they don't have an emergency fund.[6]

6. Laura Wronski. "CNBC | Momentive Your Money Financial Confidence Survey," CNBC Momentive. April 11, 2023. https://www.momentive.ai/en/blog/cnbc-financial-literacy-2023/.

IV.
ARE YOU READY FOR
FINANCIAL SUCCESS?

You have probably heard your mother say, "That money is burning a hole in your pocket, and you just can't wait to spend it!" One of the keys to financial success is to be comfortable with money to the point where you don't feel like you have to spend it. If you don't have your mindset right for money, money won't solve your problems.

You have to ask yourself if you're ready for financial success. Would you be able to receive a large sum of money and have the discipline not to splurge on material things?

Income tax returns, for example. Many people I know already have their income tax return spent before they get it. They already know what they're going to splurge on and exactly what they're going to buy. Rarely does it include saving that money and then spending it on something that will make them more money.

Years ago, I purchased an investment property. A gentleman, let's call him Jose, bought the home from me as an owner-financed property. I paid $34,000 for the property, and invested $10,000 in improvements for a total investment of $44,000. It was a three-bedroom, one bath, 950-square foot residential property in a decent neighborhood. Jose saved his income tax returns for four years to have the down payment for the home. I sold the property to Jose for $64,000. Jose paid off the home in eight years, paying me $78,000 with interest. That home is now valued at almost $200,000, Jose owns it free and clear, and it's valued at $122,000 more than he paid for it.

Having money gives you access to things you may not be ready for. I'm sure you can name a lot of famous people that were rich but not successful in life because they spent their money as soon as they got it and were not able to maintain that lifestyle. If money was the key to everything, many of the famous people you named likely wouldn't have problems. Unfortunately, you can probably name quite a few famous people who were rich but passed away due to suicide or excessive use of drugs or alcohol. I'm certainly not insinuating that your situation is this dire, but what I am saying, is the key to success with having money is to get comfortable with not spending it as soon as you get it.

I remember a friend of mine who was injured as a kid and received a substantial settlement through a lawsuit when he turned eighteen. When he received that money, he gained access to things he wasn't ready for (drugs, alcohol, etc). Instead of marijuana, he started buying crack cocaine. He was able to afford things he wasn't ready for. Having money put him in circles and around people and things he wasn't ready for, and his inability to manage money ruined his life.

People often come to me and ask me to help them with their credit score. The first thing I ask is, "Are you ready for a good credit score?"

What that means is are you financially responsible enough for the things having a "good credit score" will afford? Are you ready to have money and maintain a high quality of life without spending your money on things that don't contribute to your success or things that don't have value?

For example, a 750 credit score will likely get you access to the house you want. But are you ready to maintain that home? Home maintenance can be incredibly expensive. Now that you have the house, do you have $5,000 in the bank in case your AC unit goes out? That's what I mean by being ready for success. You have the house, but if you can't maintain it, you're not ready for it.

Here are a few other examples of not being ready for success:

Living paycheck to paycheck - "I got paid today. I didn't even realize today was payday" vs. "I won't go to the mall until Friday, because I don't get paid until Friday."

Being comfortable with money means you don't feel like you need to run out and spend it as soon as you get it.

Lottery winners - Studies show that a significant number of lottery winners spend the majority of their winnings or file for bankruptcy within five years.[7]

Professional athletes - According to *Sports Illustrated*, 78% of NFL players face financial trouble within two years of leaving the game, and 60% of NBA players are in the same boat five years after retirement. On average, NFL players last 3.3 years in the league, while NHL, NBA, and

---

7. Rebecca Lake. "Lottery Winner Statistics: 23 Eye Popping Facts," Credit Donkey. August 11, 2022. https://www.creditdonkey.com/lottery-winner-statistics.html.

MLB careers last 3.5, 4.8, and 5.6 years, respectively.[8] Professional athletes often spend their money on big houses, cars, and other material things, but they also tend to spend their money on family, friends and bad investments.

Family & friends - We all have family and friends that we love and certainly want to be in a position to help out during their times of need. However, it's extremely important to have financial boundaries to make sure when you have money, you don't lose it all by giving and lending to family and friends or making bad investments.

Years ago, I came home on holiday leave and went to visit one of my old Army buddies. I got to his home and walked in, and he and his family were sitting in the dark with candles lit.

I asked him, "What's going on?"

He said, "Oh man, I couldn't pay the electric bill."

His bill was around $200. I gave him the money to pay his bill so he and his family wouldn't be in the dark. That was money I gave him not expecting to get it back. I had that money to give him, not because I was rich, but because I managed my money well.

There are some of my friends or family members who know they cannot borrow money from me because at some point in the past they have proven that they won't pay me (or others) back; they have not been truthful about why they needed money; or they have shown me that they

---

8. Pablo Torre. "How and Why Athletes Go Broke," Sports Illustrated, March 23, 2009. https://vault.si.com/vault/2009/03/23/how-and-why-athletes-go-broke.

will spend their money on Air Jordan shoes and Gucci handbags, but then ask me for money to pay their rent. That's not how this works.

Here are a few tips on creating financial boundaries for family and friends:

- Set limits on *what* you are willing to lend money for and *how much* money you're willing to lend.
- Never loan what you're not willing to lose.
- If a friend or family member comes to you with a business prospect and wants you to invest, treat it like you're a bank making a business decision. Ask yourself, "If this person were not my family member, would I lend them money?"
- Make sure the person that's asking for money has some skin in the game. For example, if my sister is trying to buy a car that's $4,000, and she has saved $3,200 and asks me for $800, then as long as she has a plan to repay me, I'm likely to lend her the $800. In this case, she has skin in the game and she's shown that she is serious by saving almost all of what she needs to buy the car. This would be a different scenario if she came to me and said she had $1,000, the car costs $4,000, and she needs to borrow $3,000. In this scenario, I would have more skin in the game than she does. I'm more likely to tell her to come back after she has saved $3,000 and I will loan her the rest.
- Be leery of anyone who always participates in "get rich quick schemes" or "quick credit fixes."

The key to ALL of this is to become responsible enough to have money, not spend it as soon as you get it, and learn how to manage it when you have it.

Question: When, not if, you become successful at managing your money, how will you keep it?

Here's What Worked for Me ...

Restrict your access. Put your money in a money market account that requires multiple steps to withdraw money (i.e., it takes two to three days to withdraw funds; can't withdraw without penalty; no debit card for the account so you have to actually go to the bank to withdraw funds; etc). These things are inconvenient and will help control the impulse to spend.

Let others hold or handle your money. If you have substantial assets, hire a financial advisor to help you make decisions on spending significant amounts of money.

Ask someone you trust to keep your money in a savings account for a specific purpose until you save enough to achieve that purpose (Tip: make sure this is a person who doesn't need your money, and will hold you accountable for withdrawing the money early or spending it on something other than your stated purpose). I have been that person in my family that others have asked to hold their money, and my wife has for her family members as well.

Set financial boundaries for giving and lending to family and friends. It's certainly okay to share your blessings with family and friends, but keep it simple, and make it make sense.

What are your **top three takeaways** from this chapter?

How will you change or maintain your mindset to achieve financial success?

_____

_____

_____

_____

_____

_____

_____

_____

_____

_____

_____

_____

_____

_____

_____

_____

_____

_____

_____

_____

_____

_____

_____

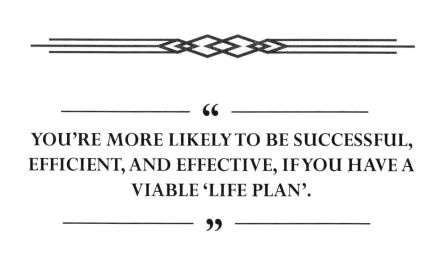

YOU'RE MORE LIKELY TO BE SUCCESSFUL, EFFICIENT, AND EFFECTIVE, IF YOU HAVE A VIABLE 'LIFE PLAN'.

Jbm Seminars

The TIAA Institute and George Washington University report that financial literacy is positively correlated with retirement planning, suggesting that those with higher financial literacy are more likely to plan for their future.[9]

---

9. Andrea Hasler, Annamaria Lusardi, Paul Yakoboski, "Financial Literacy, Longevity Literacy and Retirement Readiness," TIAA Institute, January 12, 2023. https://www.tiaa.org/public/institute/publication/2023/financial_literacy_longevity_literacy_and_retirement_readiness.

V.

DEVELOP YOUR LIFE PLAN

Almost every successful business, organization, or team has a "plan for success." You're more likely to be successful, efficient, and effective if you have a viable "life plan." If you fail to plan, you're planning to fail. This chapter is designed to give you the tools to develop a plan for your entire life, and execute it.

Five Components of a Life Plan

I.   Health
II. Finances (Budget, Credit Score, Savings)
III. Career/Education
IV. Family
V.   Spiritual Guidance

Let's talk about each in detail.

I. HEALTH

The most important aspect of your life plan is your health. If you're not in good health, it could lead to difficulties in many other areas of your life. Do you know your optimal blood pressure, optimal weight, blood sugar, cholesterol level, etc? If you don't, what is your plan to find out? On your next visit for your annual physical, talk to your doctor and determine if you're in your optimal zones. If you're not in your optimal zones, your doctor can provide guidance and instruction on how to achieve and maintain optimal health zones.

MINDSET CHECK v

It's YOUR responsibility to take care of yourself. Get an annual check-up; eat well; get regular exercise, and see a nutritionist if necessary. You can have all the money in the world, but if you don't have good health, it won't matter.

II. FINANCES

The next step in your life plan is to understand your finances. Do you have a budget? Do you have six to nine months living expenses saved? Are you preparing for retirement? Do you know your credit score and what's on your credit report? As previously mentioned, you can obtain one free copy of your credit report once a year from Experian, Equifax, and TransUnion.

https://www.annualcreditreport.com/index.action

The Credit Karma app is a good tool to monitor your credit on a daily basis. Credit Karma doesn't give you your actual credit score or report; however, it is a great summary of the major items that appear on your credit report, and it is a good estimate of your credit score.
https://www.creditkarma.com/

These are all critical factors of your life plan. I break down budgeting, credit score, and savings in great detail under the Financial Plan discussion in Chapter VI.

III. EDUCATION/CAREER

Education:

The educational aspect of your life should be planned. Lack of planning sets you up for failure.

For example, if you spend $120,000 on a degree, but you didn't realize that the salary in your degree field maxes out at $50,000, it will be difficult for you to realize a return on your investment.

During high school and college, you should be thinking about your future. You must understand that the decisions you make in one phase of your life will affect the next phase. If you're in high school, or your child is in high school, it's imperative that you and/or your child begin making decisions about going to college. Ask yourself these questions:

- What is your area of study?
- What is the return on the investment?
- How much will it cost?
- Exactly how will you pay for it?

– Plan your education beyond high school so that you can get in, get out and start your career - that's the goal. Don't be a "career student."

– Know if your career path will require an advanced degree to be successful (i.e., doctors and lawyers must complete undergraduate and graduate studies to pursue this career field).

– Know exactly how you're going to pay for your education. Are your grades and test scores high enough to get academic scholarships? Will you need a loan? Will you join the military? Will you be able to get an athletic scholarship?

– If you're going to further your education, the costs will hit your budget now, or in the future.

Career:

"What's next?"

Once you finish your education and begin working in your career field, ask yourself what's next? What's your next promotion, next raise, next step in leadership, next certification, etc. You should always work towards what's next. You should strive for your next position and chart your path to get there.

If there is a ceiling you can't break through in your current location, division, or career field, consider relocating or switching industries to get to the next level. If your career has an earning ceiling, and you want to earn more, you have to invest in yourself and develop a skill set that will allow you to grow and achieve that next step.

So often, people don't take the time to invest in themselves to get that certification or degree that will allow them to advance. Your plan should include your current career status and how long you plan to remain at that level. If you want to move to the next step, you have to identify what you need to do to get to the next level and how long that will take.

IV. FAMILY

One of my beliefs in life is that without family or a support system, you are less likely to be successful. It is critical to have a support system of family and friends. Trying to be successful alone is often more difficult. The family unit is critical, but you must learn to navigate your family and be successful in your environment.

I would not be as successful if I did not have family structure and support. However, you have to identify those family members and friends that support you and those who may slow your progress. If you're like me and grew up in a large family without a lot of money, you probably understand that many family members in this situation can be interdependent on each other for life necessities (i.e., borrowing your car, asking for money to pay bills, etc.).

You have to be able to create boundaries for some family members to ensure your success. It's okay to assist your family, but understand where that line needs to be. You may be more than willing to help a family member pay an electric bill if they lost their job, but not when they don't have money to pay their bills because they spent their money on new gym shoes. Sometimes, you simply have to love them from a distance.

V. SPIRITUAL GUIDANCE

I'm not going to get too deep in this book about the spiritual realm; however, you should have a higher being that you believe in and can call on to assist you during your time in need, including managing your finances and managing your life. If you want to explore spiritual principles, there is a great book by David and Debbie Bragonier that teaches the use of scripture to manage your money.[10]

I encourage you to pray for guidance, knowledge, and wisdom, and pray for signs that will give you strength to endure and accomplish certain things in your life. I advocate for meditating, understanding your purpose, and understanding how to achieve peace in your life. Financial freedom brings peace in your life. The two go hand in hand. You should also study your spiritual teachings and nurture your relationship with your higher power by attending church services, or whatever your teachings dictate, on a regular basis.

This is not a step that you can skip. Remember, the most important aspect of this financial journey is your mindset.

---

10. David and Debbie Bragonier with Kimn S. Gollnick. *Getting Your Financial House in Order: A Floorplan for Managing Your Money*, B & H Pub Group, 2003.

You must have a spiritual plan in place for your life. It will assist you when things get difficult and increase your chances for success.

You must have a higher power to help you get your mind right as you embark on this journey. You will need spiritual guidance. Financial discipline is more than a notion.

What are your **top three takeaways** from this chapter?

_____

_____

_____

Write Your Life Plan:

Health: _____

_____

_____

_____

Finances: _____

_____

_____

_____

Career/Education: _____

_____

_____

_____

Family: _____

_____

_____

_____

Spiritual Guidance: _____

_____

_____

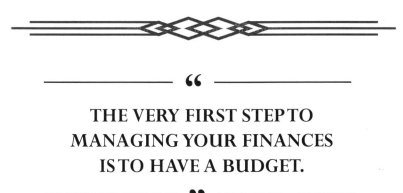

"

THE VERY FIRST STEP TO
MANAGING YOUR FINANCES
IS TO HAVE A BUDGET.

"

Jbm Seminars

The Global Financial Literacy Excellence Center reports that a Standard & Poor's Ratings Services Global Financial Literacy Survey found that only 57% of adults in the United States are financially literate.[11]

11. "S & P Global Financial Literacy Survey," Global Financial Literacy Excellence Center, Accessed September 3, 2023. https://gflec.org/initiatives/sp-global-finlit-survey-2/.

VI.
FINANCIAL PLAN
(BUDGET/CREDIT SCORE/SAVINGS)

CONGRATULATIONS! If you've reached this point in the book, you've already taken the first step to changing your mindset! No matter what level of success you've achieved or haven't achieved the VERY FIRST STEP to managing your finances is to have a budget. You must have a budget – it doesn't matter if you're making $200,000 a year or $25,000 a year. Your budget is the key!

A. CREATING YOUR BUDGET

Include the following components in your budget based on the percentage (%) of your monthly NET pay (not gross). The goal is to have 100%, but the ranges give you flexibility to make adjustments.

Housing (Home) – 25-30% – No more than 25-30% of your income should be dedicated to your home

Transportation – 10-15%

Insurance (life, health, vehicle) – 10-20%

Food – 5-10%

Utilities – 5-10%

Charitable Giving – 10%

Personal – 5-10%

Entertainment/Recreation – 5-10%

Medical – 5-10%

Clothing – 2-5%

Savings – 10%

MISC

Example. This simple graphic is for illustration purposes only based on net pay of $3,000 per month:

Sample Budget

$3000 Monthly Net Pay

Rent	$1200	
Car	$350	
Car Insurance	$150	
Food	$300	
Utilities	$150	
Phone Cable internet	$200	
Clothes	$75	
Insurance	$100	
Savings/investments	$400	= $2925

If you follow a budget, it's difficult to fail. Where many people fail is if they want something outside of the budget, they will spend more than they are supposed to and bust the budget to get what they want.

You may not always be able to drive the car you want, or live in the neighborhood you want, or you may need a roommate to make ends meet. You get off track when you live beyond your means.

When I was twenty-two years old, I had very limited income, and lived with two other roommates in a townhome to make it work. This worked for my budget at the time, so this is what I had to do. You must learn how to live within your budget to create a mindset of living within your means.

B. BREAKING DOWN YOUR CREDIT SCORE

Financial institutions use credit scores as a model to determine your credit worthiness. Your credit score is not as important as you think, but it's as important as you think. Confused? Let me explain. People try to improve their credit score, but haven't changed the behavior that led to a bad credit score.

I often hear people say, "I want to raise my credit score to buy a house."

The first thing you need to talk about is how got you a 580 credit score. Paying a credit services company to improve your score without solving the behavior won't help you long term. With an improved credit score, you can buy the house, but you won't be mentally prepared to maintain it. If you solve the behavior, you will solve the problem, and your credit score will go up with time. If you're paying off your credit cards, the utilization will go down; in turn, your score will go up. If you're still making bad decisions, your score will go down again.

Your mindset and actions that got you in trouble in the first place are what you need to focus on. Hence, it's really not as important as you think, but it's as important as you think. Time is always your friend. The longer your credit report reflects good credit history, the better.

C. UNDERSTANDING YOUR CREDIT SCORE

According to a 2019 study by the *New York Post*, one in eight Americans are unaware of their credit score.[12] Credit scores are generally between 300-850.

FICO Score – In the financial industry, a FICO score is the same as a credit score.

The three major credit reporting agencies are:

Equifax
TransUnion
Experian

All three reporting agencies generally give different scores. Banks use different algorithms to determine your score. If a bank pulls your credit report, the bank generally throws out the high score and the low score from the three reporting agencies and uses your middle score.

---

12. Zoya Gervis. "Shocking Percentage of Americans Don't Know Their Credit Score," New York Post, December 17, 2019. https://nypost. com/2019/12/17/shocking-percentage-of-americans-dont-know-their-credit-score/.

Example–Your scores:

Equifax	680
TransUnion	720
Experian	750
The bank will go with	*720*

Credit Karma - This service does not provide your true credit score, but it can be used as a guideline for your estimated score. Visit their website at www.creditkarma.com for more information.

Note: *Vantage Score* - There is a new scoring model called Vantage Score 4.0, and it uses different algorithms than the FICO scores. If your bank uses the Vantage Score, do your research on how that will affect your score.

Example of a scoring model for rating credit scores*

640-670 – Average
671-710 – Good
711-749 – Very good
750 and above – Excellent

* Rating credit scores is highly subjective. Financial institutions use different algorithms and different scoring models for guidance. Numbers may vary.

What makes up the credit score?[13]
Five important factors – "35, 30, 15, 10 & 10"

---

13. "What's In My FICO Scores?" myFico.com, Accessed September 3, 2023. https://www.myfico.com/credit-education/whats-in-your-credit-score.

Payment History	35%
Credit Utilization (amounts owed)	30%
Length of Credit History	15%
Type of Credit (credit mix)	10%
Inquiries (new credit)	10%

1. *Payment history* - This is 35% of your score. Late payments stay on your report for seven years.

2. *Credit Utilization* - This is 30% of your score. Don't exceed 20% usage of the credit limit per month (Example - If you have a $1,000 limit, you should not carry more than a $200 balance).

3. *Length of Credit History* - This is 15% of your credit score. You should not close a credit card you've had for ten years. You will lose ten years of credit history. I recommend leaving the card open and keeping the usage below 20% of utilization. You will need to use it every now and then and pay the balance each month before the closing date. If there is no activity on a card for an extended

period of time, the company may close the card, which could negatively affect your score. The longer you have the card in good standing, the better it will be for your credit score.

4. *Type of Credit* - The categories of credit you have make up 10% of your score. Banks want to see that you have diverse credit, either revolving or installment and in good standing. You need a mix of credit to show that you can manage and maintain it (mortgage, car, credit cards, loans etc.)

   —Installment example - mortgage, or car payment; which is a fixed amount
   —Revolving example - credit card; the amount can change every month; not a fixed amount

5. *Recent Credit Inquiries* – Inquiries make up 10% of your score

   —Soft inquiry – Generally will not affect your score. This is like you checking your score on Credit Karma.

   —Hard inquiry – Would be a bank or lending institute pulling your credit. They must get your permission to pull your credit. This will affect your score.

As a general rule, limit the number of businesses from which you try to obtain credit. Multiple inquiries can lower your credit score; however, like inquiries are generally not counted against you.

For example, if you are in the market to buy a home, and you have three different mortgage companies pull your credit within a two-week period, it will count as one inquiry and won't damage your score. However, if you have a mortgage company, car dealership, and furniture store pull your credit within a short amount of time, it will count as three separate inquiries and will lower your credit score.

Takeaways:

Do you know your credit score? What is it? _____

Why is your credit score so important?

Your credit score affects the interest rate you pay on a loan. If your score is low, you could end up paying double over the life of the loan.

For example, you could end up paying $144,000 more than another person with the same loan amount on a house. They will get a better interest rate due to their high credit score.

Wait until your score is considered excellent to get the best interest rate. Then buy your house!

How to improve your credit score or establish credit:

Unsecured Credit Card

—Requires a good credit score
—The credit limit is generally between $200 - $1,000
—Make small purchases on the card every month
—Pay off the balance in full each month before closing date
—Don't exceed 20% usage of the credit limit
—Never miss a payment and don't make late payments

Secured Credit Card

—$200 minimum down to secure the card
—Your limit is usually how much you put down
—Banks will generally offer these as an option
—Make small purchases on the card every month
—Pay off the balance in full each month before closing date
—Don't exceed 20% usage of the credit limit
—Never miss a payment and don't make late payments

If you handle it correctly, the bank will generally turn your secured card into an unsecured card.

Authorized User

— Become an authorized user
— Piggyback off of someone else's good credit
— Don't use the card unless that's the plan
— Don't use EINs or another person's SSN (it's illegal)
— Do this for your kids going to college

For example, make your children authorized users on your credit card, and you pay the bill each month on time. This will help them build credit so that when they get out of college, they will walk away with great credit history and a good credit score. This will also help them understand how to stay within a budget.

Check Your Credit Report and Dispute Errors

— Use www.annualcreditreport.com to monitor your credit
— The three major credit reporting bureaus report to www.annualcreditreport.com
— You are entitled to one report each year from each agency
— There are a lot of fancy ways to do this, but it's easy to just go online and dispute any errors. Again, you don't have to pay someone to do this for you.

Identify two to three things that you can charge to your credit card consistently each month and immediately pay off before the closing date (ex. groceries, lunch, gas, dinner, etc.)

Remember, the key to building good credit is to demonstrate responsible credit utilization.

_____

_____

_____

_____

_____

_____

_____

_____

_____

_____

D. SAVINGS

When I was younger and people said, "You have to save money," my response was, "I'm tapped out." In order to save money, I realized I had to find money that I was giving away. I was broke and had zero dollars in my savings account. I had to figure out a way to increase my savings.

I tried going "cold turkey" and not spend money on anything except necessities. This didn't work for long. I wanted to get my life together, but I also wanted to enjoy my life. I finally figured out I had to find a way to save money, but at the same time enjoy the fruits of my labor.

Back to the plan.

You must have a plan to save because it's one of the hardest things to do.

Establish an emergency fund:

If you have not been successful at saving in the past, or if your savings is less than $500, this is a great place to start.

I started by saving $400 for five months to establish an emergency fund of $2,000. Once I established an emergency fund, I could look to pay off debt. I didn't try to pay off debt before I had an emergency fund because if something came up, I would only have debt and no savings.

Finding money you already have or money that you're giving away:

I increased my withholdings on my W4 to go from zero exemptions to one exemption. This reduced my tax liability and allowed me to save the difference. For example, if I paid $150 in taxes per pay period ($300 per month), then increased my exemptions, I would only pay $75 per period ($150 per month), giving me with the ability to save and/or invest the $150 I saved in tax liability.

NOTE: You will get less of an income tax return at the end of the year, but you will actually get it monthly instead of in January after you file your taxes.

Please consult your tax professional before changing your exemptions.

Raise your insurance deductible:

According to insurance companies that process data for William Mattar Law Offices, on average a person will have an at-fault car accident every eighteen years. That averages out to four accidents in their entire lifetime.[14]

We're all afraid of having an accident and paying a high deductible. But the data shows the likelihood of having an at-fault accident only occurs about once every other decade. Since there was a low risk of having an accident where I may be at fault, I increased the deductible and put the money that I was saving by not paying a high deductible in my savings account.

For example: When I increased my deductible from $250 to $500, I saved $75 per month on my premium. $75 per month x 12 is $900 a year. I took that money and put it in a savings account. If I only had an at-fault accident about once every other decade, that meant I was saving $9,000 in a decade. To complain about not paying a deductible that is $250 higher doesn't make sense when you can save $9,000 over ten years.

In the event you have an accident and have to pay the higher deductible, you should feel more comfortable because you have the money to pay a higher deductible since you already saved it. In a year, you doubled that amount.

---

14. "How Many Car Accidents Does the Average Person Have?" William Matter Law Offices, November 20, 2020. https://www.williammattar.com/blog/car-accident/how-many-car-accidents-does-the-average-person-have/.

Cut down on social events:

I saved $175 per month by reducing my spending on general entertainment and social events like movies, clubbing, and eating out.

- I stopped going to the movies every weekend and went every other weekend.
- I started going to the club before 11:00pm when entry was free.
- I started cooking more and eating out less.

Snowball Your Debt:

The best way for me to pay off my debt was to "snowball" it. After establishing an emergency fund, I took the disposable income that I was saving from the reductions from taxes and insurance premium and paid off my credit card debt one at a time. I started with the lowest credit card debt and paid that off. Then, I moved to the next credit card with the lowest balance and paid that one off. After that, I moved to the next credit card with the lowest balance and paid that one off, and so on, until all the debt was paid off.

Overall, this process took me a year and a half to pay off all of my credit cards. I went from $400 a month of disposable income to $600 a month of disposable income, and I started saving the difference. This is what went to my savings account to achieve the emergency fund. Do you see how it all works together?

Saving six to nine months of living expenses:

Once you have done all of that, you're now ready to start the maintenance phase. Add up all of your monthly living expenses (you should already have this number from creating your budget) and multiply it by nine. This is the minimum amount of money you should have on hand in your savings account at all times. What's your number?

Monthly living expenses: $_____

x 9 months = $_____

Saving six to nine months of living expenses will eliminate a lot of stress in your life if you lose your job, have a major issue with your home, or need to replace or repair a vehicle.

Please understand this process is building your emergency fund. It's not to be dipped into every time you get an itch to buy something or want to pay for the family Disney vacation. It is for true emergencies.

If you have to use these funds, you also have to replenish the fund. Having an emergency fund will give you enough time to look for another job that will satisfy you instead of taking whatever is available.

It's time to put everything you've learned into action and do your 7 DAY FINANCIAL FAST! Choose your days and start the fast. Others have done it, and you can too!

"I did the 7 DAY FINANCIAL fast during jbmseminars online financial workshop. Total transparency - I learned a lot about myself and the way I spend money. I actually struggled to not spend money. I failed the first two days. I committed to seven days and I will finish strong. I've actually saved money and it felt good."

—Jacqueline Jones, Chicago, IL

7 DAY FINANCIAL FAST!

— Only buy necessities
— Don't eat out
— Take your lunch to work, school, etc
— Don't shop online

Fasting Days: _____ to _____

How many days were you successful with your financial fast? _____

Which category did you spend most of your money on?

_____

What did you learn about yourself and your spending habits?

_____

_____

_____

_____

_____

_____

_____

How will you change or maintain your mindset to achieve financial success?

_____

_____

_____

_____

_____

_____

_____

If you didn't make it through seven days, commit and try again.

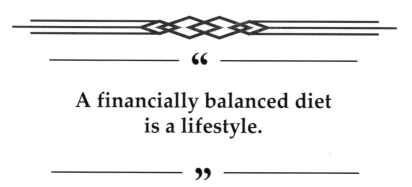

A financially balanced diet
is a lifestyle.

Jbm Seminars

A 2023 Retirement Confidence Survey by the Employee Benefit Research Institute found that 32% of Americans who were surveyed report that the total value of their savings for retirement and investments, excluding the value of their primary home, is less than $25,000.[15]

15. "2023 Retirement Confidence Survey, Fact Sheet #3, Preparing for Retirement In America," Employee Benefit Research Institute, Accessed September 10, 2023. https://www.ebri.org/docs/default-source/rcs/2023-rcs/rcs_23-fs-3_prep.pdf?sfvrsn=778d392f_4.

VII.

THE 1/3 FINANCIAL SYSTEM

Think of the 1/3 System like a balanced diet...a financially balanced diet. A financially balanced diet is a lifestyle.

Take your monthly disposable income, and split it three ways.

In simple terms, the 1/3 Financial System allows you to Spend 1/3 | Save 1/3 | Invest 1/3

Example:

- Spend 1/3 - Increase standard of living with moderation (treat yourself once a week/month)
- Save 1/3 - Money market account
- Invest 1/3 - Roth IRA, 401k, real estate, stocks

Note: Withdrawing funds early from an IRA, 401k or any type of retirement account may have serious tax implications. Please visit with your tax professional prior to making an early withdrawal.

I explained earlier that I tried to go cold turkey and save all of my money and only spend money on necessities. Most people who do this will fall off the wagon because they're saving all of their money but not enjoying life and experiencing the fruits of their labor. That's exactly what happened to me. In changing my mindset, I started thinking about how I could save money and still make my money make money. I used the 1/3 System for every bonus, every pay raise, and any money I saved. In about seven years, I had $100,000 savings in the bank.

Once I saved $100,000, I started thinking about how I could use that money to make more money. This is what took me to the next level. When you have this kind of success, know you've done the work, and changed your mindset to become financially healthy, your confidence goes through the roof. Based on my plan, I knew real estate investing would be my next move. While I was changing my behavior, I started researching and learning everything I could about real estate investments so that when I got the money, I would be ready to invest.

Investing in real estate allowed me to establish disposable and residual income and accumulate wealth. Then I was able to save a substantial down payment and increase my net worth to the amount required to invest in the Quiznos franchise. This was not an easy task. It took time, discipline, and effort, but it was well worth it to see the fruits of my labor pay off.

MINDSET CHECK √

What are your **three takeaways** from this chapter?

How will you change or maintain your mindset to achieve financial success?

_____

_____

_____

_____

_____

_____

_____

What is your plan for spending 1/3, saving 1/3 and investing 1/3?

Monthly disposable income: $_____

Spend 1/3: $_____

Save 1/3: $_____

Invest 1/3: $_____

Types of investments:

_____

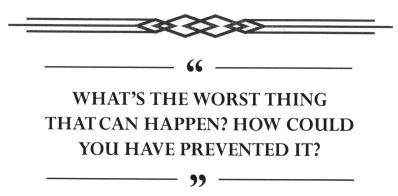

WHAT'S THE WORST THING THAT CAN HAPPEN? HOW COULD YOU HAVE PREVENTED IT?

Jbm Seminars

According to a recent Forbes Advisory survey on life insurance, 48% of Americans do not have life insurance.[16]

---

16. Chauncey Crail, "Life Insurance Statistics, Data and Industry Trends 2023," Forbes Advisor, June 21, 2023. https://www.forbes.com/advisor/life-insurance/life-insurance-statistics/#:~:text=The%20percentage%20of%20Americans%20with,life%20insurance%2C%20according%20to%20LIMRA.

VIII.

RISK ASSESSMENT

There is risk in every aspect of life. Assessing financial risk means being prepared for life's challenges and surprises. In assessing financial risk, you need to ask yourself these questions:

— What's the worst thing that can happen?
— How can I prevent it?
— And even if I try to prevent it, and it happens anyway, what's my Plan B?

Example - Let's say you and your spouse are on a trip driving across the country. *What's the worst thing that can happen?* You can have an accident. Let's break this down.
How could you have prevented the accident?

— Drive the speed limit
— Get enough sleep
— Being a defensive driver
— Making sure your vehicle has proper maintenance

Your risk of having an accident drops considerably when you take preventative steps to avoid challenging circumstances. Let's say you did all of those things, and you still had an accident. *What's your Plan B?*

— Proper insurance
— Have an emergency contact to assist you
  right away
— Have additional funds in case you have to rent
  a car to continue with your trip

If you do these things in most situations, you will reduce your financial risk considerably. Having money solves most issues because you can get yourself out of most binds with money. But if you do the risk assessment, it will likely prevent you from spending money unnecessarily.

Example - A friend of mine drove from Chicago to Dallas and got a flat tire. He went to the tire shop to get the flat changed, but was told he actually needed four new tires and he wouldn't make it back to Chicago if he didn't get his tires changed. The problem was he didn't have the money to buy four new tires. A risk assessment before he left Chicago would have clued him in that he needed new tires so he likely would have chosen a different mode of travel or had his tires changed before he left Chicago.

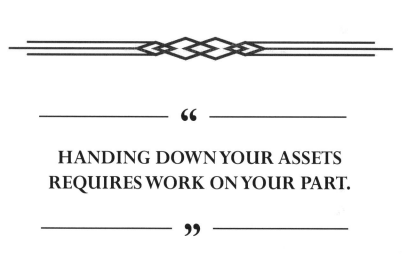

"

**HANDING DOWN YOUR ASSETS
REQUIRES WORK ON YOUR PART.**

"

Jbm Seminars

The Financial Literacy Crisis in America 2023 Report by Ramsey Education finds that 88% of U.S. adults didn't feel prepared to handle money after graduating high school.[17]

17. "The Financial Literacy Crisis in America 2023 Report by Ramsey Education," Yahoo Finance, April 3, 2023. https://finance.yahoo.com/news/financial-literacy-crisis-america-2023-100000912.html.

IX.

LEGACY BUILDING

Legacy Building is choosing how your assets will be handed down and who you will hand them down to. Handing down assets to your loved ones requires work on your part. The first step is to have a legacy mindset.

For example, consider the game of Monopoly. It teaches a legacy mindset in how owning and acquiring land as an asset works to your advantage. This is a great tool to teach your kids about retaining wealth.

In Monopoly, if you roll the dice and land on someone else's property, you will owe them rent. Whereas, if you own the land, and someone lands on your property, they will have to pay *you*. The general concept is those who own the most property usually win the game.

Part of your job in building your legacy is to identify who you will leave your assets to; however, education is the key to asset retention. Educate your heirs on how to manage money. This will prevent them from squandering everything you've spent a lifetime building in six months.

Things to Consider:
Financial literacy early and often
  — Identify those who can correctly manage money
  — Take the emotional aspect out of the decision
    (even though you love your family members,
    some of them may not be the best money managers)

— Establish a trust and name those individuals in the trust

Examples of things you can do to build your family legacy:

— Pay for college expenses for your children and other young people in your family that you have identified
— Give them a down payment toward their first home or investment property as a gift instead of paying for a wedding
— If you own a business, hire qualified family members to work for you and learn your business. Pay them a market salary and give them a decision-making position with responsibility

ESTATE PLANNING *

This section is designed to provide you with general concepts on estate planning. I do not have expertise in estate planning. Please visit with an estate planning attorney, financial planner, or certified public accountant for advice and guidance on estate planning.

Having an estate plan is the best way to protect your assets and ensure your legacy continues after your death.

Living Trust - A living trust allows you to transfer property to the people and charities of your choice, generally without going through probate.

Will - A will is a legal document that directs the disposition of your assets after your death.

Power of Attorney (POA) - A written authorization to represent or act on another's behalf in private affairs, business, finances, medical affairs, or some other designated legal matter. The POA is effective in the event the represented party becomes incapacitated or dies.

Online Resources:
- SuzeOrman.com (will and trust)
- Legalzoom.com
- Moneycrashers.com

Here's What Worked for Me ...

I established a 529 Savings Plans for my grandkids.

529 Savings Plan – **An investment plan that enables you to save money for a beneficiary and pay for education expenses**. You can save money on an after-tax basis and withdraw funds tax-free to cover nearly any type of college expense. When you withdraw the money for qualified educational expenses, you won't pay any taxes on the gains, either.[18]

Types of 529 Plans:
— College savings plan
— Prepaid tuition plan

The college savings plan allows earnings to grow tax-deferred and withdrawals are tax-free when used for qualified education expenses. Most states offer at least one of these plans.

---

18. Julia Kagan, "529 Plan: What It Is, How It Works, Pros and Cons," Investopedia, August 23, 2023. https://www.investopedia.com/terms/1/529plan.asp.

Prepaid tuition plans allow the account owner to pay current tuition rates for future attendance at designated colleges and universities. That means most likely, you can lock in a lower cost of college attendance. There are many other outside-of-the-box things you can do to produce income to help pay for college.

STUDENT OWNERSHIP OF INVESTMENT PROPERTY

If you start saving money for your child when they're born, by the time that child goes to college, you could have enough money to purchase an investment property in the city your child will attend college. This will create revenue, and has the potential to offset rent, create residual income, and make your student a property owner at an early age.

TEACH YOUR CHILDREN MONEY MANAGEMENT EARLY

Allow your children to manage money early. For example, your child's allowance may be $100 per month. Their expenses may be lunch, going to movies with friends, or self-care. Chances are this amount will not last the full month. If not, instead of the parents giving them more money, the child should have to do what adults do - adjust until their allowance gets replenished. This will teach them to stay within their budget. This may be a difficult lesson for your child to learn, but this will allow them to fail under your umbrella, so that when they go off on their own, it won't be the first time they have failed in managing money. Kids learn more from their failures. This teaches them at an early age to budget for what they need and adjust when they over spend.

MINDSET CHECK √

What are your **top three takeaways** from this chapter?

How will you change or maintain your mindset to achieve financial success?

_____

_____

_____

_____

_____

_____

_____

_____

_____

_____

_____

_____

_____

- -

- -

- -

- -

- -

- -

- -

- -

> " YOU MUST BE IN THE RIGHT
> MINDSET TO MAKE YOUR
> FINANCIAL DREAMS A REALITY. "

Jbm Seminars

A 2023 study by the Lincoln Financial Group shows that people who set specific financial goals are two to three times more likely to see improvement in their personal finances.[19]

---

19. "New Lincoln Financial Group study reports one in three Americans struggles financially, but goal-setting is a game-changer," Lincoln Financial Group, February 1, 2023. https://newsroom.lfg.com/new-lincoln-financial-group-study-reports-one-in-three-americans-struggles-financially-but-goal-setting-is-game-changer.htm.

X.

"MINDSET MATTERS"
25 THINGS THAT HAVE NOTHING TO DO WITH MONEY, BUT HAVE EVERYTHING TO DO WITH MONEY

"**M**indset Matters" are things that have *nothing* to do with money, but have *everything* to do with money. These are best practices to implement on a daily basis to keep you on track and in the right mindset to make your financial dreams a reality. These concepts have helped me maintain financial freedom and success for the last thirty years. Try it my way; modify it to fit your lifestyle, whatever works for you. Just get started and remember, the key to financial success is...

Mindset First Money Second.

1. SET S.M.A.R.T. GOALS

A "goal" is an idea of the future or desired result that a person or a group of people envision, plan, and commit to achieve.[20]

Setting goals for your life is equal to creating a roadmap to success. Goal setting is an absolute must. There are **hundreds** of books and articles you can read on how to set goals. One of the most effective ways to set goals is to use the S.M.A.R.T. Goals method.

---

20. "Goal Setting," Wikepdia, last modified June 2018, https://en.wikipedia.org/wiki/Goal.

The Corporate Finance Institute has an excellent primer on setting S.M.A.R.T. Goals. [21]

S.M.A.R.T. Goals is an acronym for goals that are:

S = Specific
M = Measurable
A = Achievable
R = Realistic
T = Time-based

Specific - Be specific with what you want to achieve.

Measurable - What evidence will prove you're making progress toward your goal?

Achievable - Your goal must be reasonably achievable within the timeframe you've set.

Realistic - Is the goal within reach, realistic, and relevant to your life purpose?

Time-based – Set a realistic time frame to achieve your goal.

TWO TYPES OF GOALS:

— Short-Term Goals
— Long-Term Goals

---

21. CFI Team, "SMART Goals: Specific, Measurable, Attainable, Realistic, Timely," Corporate Financial Institute, Accessed September 10, 2023. https://corporatefinanceinstitute.com/resources/management/smart-goal/.

Short-Term Goal Range:

    Zero to six months
    Six months to one year
    One year to three years

Long-Term Goal Range:

    Three to five years
    Five to seven years
    Seven to ten years

This may seem like a lot, but time moves quickly and you need a roadmap to stay on track.

Example of setting S.M.A.R.T. Goals:

Short-Term Goal:

Specific= Get promoted to senior manager with pay increase

Measurable= High rated evaluations; increase sales; leadership training; successfully manage two high profile projects

Achievable= Received junior-level promotion in the last three years indicating you're on the promotion track

Realistic= This goal is in line with my overall values and can realistically be achieved given the available resources and time

Time-based= Two years

Long-Term Goal:

Specific=   Purchase a home
Measurable= 20% deposit saved and trackable; minimum credit score achieved; all payments made on time for two years; income to debt ratio is acceptable
Achievable= Stable employment for the last five years; median income for affording a home in my area
Realistic= This goal is in line with my overall value of becoming a homeowner
Time-based= Four years

Write down *one short-term* and *one long-term* goal using the S.M.A.R.T. Goals method:

— Identify your specific goal.
— What is the goal range?
— How will you measure your progress?
— Is the goal achievable given your circumstances?
— Is it realistic?
— What is your personal time frame for achieving your goal?

_____
_____
_____
_____
_____
_____
_____
_____

2. PLAN YOUR WEEK

One of the best ways to stay on track is to plan your entire week - Monday through Sunday. Set aside a day every week to make plans for the upcoming week. I plan my week on Sundays. Planning your week will increase your productivity, eliminate confusion about what you have to do, and keep you moving toward accomplishing your goals. Write down what you want to accomplish this week.

Monday:
Tuesday:
Wednesday:
Thursday:
Friday:
Saturday:
Sunday:

3. ELIMINATE PROCRASTINATION

Procrastination costs time and money.

You lose so much money by procrastinating. Waiting until the last minute to do things will often end up costing you more than it would if you had not waited. Procrastination doesn't just cost you money; it costs time.

Common examples of procrastination:

— Christmas-Eve shopping
— Last-minute purchasing
— Buying airline tickets less than two weeks before the flight

— Failing to plan your week
— Not taking immediate action on simple things. If something comes up, I try to take care of it immediately instead of letting it linger; if I'm driving and I can't take care of it right away, I put a voice reminder on my phone.

4. BEING LATE IS EXPENSIVE

You've probably heard a lot of your friends say, "I'm just a late person." My response - "That's BS." As a soldier in the military, I learned the importance of not being late. As the popular saying goes, "To be on time is to be late, and to be early is to be on time."

Here's What Worked for Me ...

— Give yourself a cushion. If you have an appointment that starts at 8:00am, get there at 7:30am
— Set your clock 15 minutes ahead of the actual time

When I owned my Quiznos franchise, my niece, who is my sister's daughter, used to come down from Chicago to Texas during the summer to work in my store. She would ride to work with me, but she was late one morning and she was making me late. I told my sister I was going to fire her and send her home if she didn't get her act together. My niece was shocked and asked, "Would you really fire me?"

My response: "Absolutely."

Don't be late. It could cost you your job.

5. NET WORTH & RETURN ON INVESTMENT (ROI)

Many in our community grow up not valuing or not understanding net worth, or sometimes both. Your net worth is the amount by which your assets outweigh your liabilities. If you have a six-figure salary, but never have any money left over after expenses are paid, you will still be in a bad position with no measurable net worth.

Why does it matter?

Net Worth:

For this example, let's consider a seven-figure net worth to be substantial. Having a substantial net worth can stop you from having to file for bankruptcy because you have measurable assets. Substantial net worth can be passed down to your children, nieces, nephews, etc.

Return on Investment (ROI):

The key to investments is to yield a return. In order to see a return on your investment, you will need to start or continue buying things that will make you money.

For example, if you purchase a rental property for $100,000 and every year you net $10,000 in profit, that's a 10% return on your investment. Think about how you're actually spending your money. If there is no return on your investment, ask yourself if you really need to purchase that item.

6. EMERGENCY FUND

Emergencies happen in life. There's no way around it. The question isn't if it's going to happen, the question is when is it going to happen. The difference between success and failure will be whether or not you're prepared. If you don't have an emergency fund, it's going to be very difficult to be prepared.

One day, I came home and tried to open the garage. The door didn't open. I kept hitting the button and trying to open the door, but it wouldn't open. I got out of my car and went into the house to try to open the garage from the inside, but the spring on the garage door was broken. I had to spend $500 that day to get the garage door fixed. What if I didn't have $500? Because I had an emergency fund, it was okay.

Let's say you're going along in your career and all of a sudden you get laid off, but you don't have an emergency fund. The first thing you do is try to get ANY job you can. You may be unemployed for a while, or you may be underemployed. For example, you used to make $60K a year, now you make $50K because you took the first job you could get. Your lifestyle dictates that you need a job that pays $60K to make ends meet. You're probably not living outside, but you're likely behind on your bills every month. This starts the cycle of debt and the old saying of "Robbing Peter topay Paul."

Again, the key to not drowning financially is to have six to nine months of living expenses saved. You can take your time to find the RIGHT job for you and not just the first job that comes along. The money you saved may last even longer because you will naturally cut back on spending if you're not working.

7. FINANCIAL INTIMACY

Financial intimacy defined: *Having intimate knowledge of your spouse or significant other's financial IQ, credit score, spending habits, and financial strengths and weaknesses.*

If you are in a committed relationship, it is imperative that you are knowledgeable of your partner's income. This is not something that should be kept secret if you plan to spend your life with this person. Transparency is the key. When I talk to couples with financial issues, 90% of them don't have financial intimacy. They don't know exactly how much money the other person makes, they separate their money, and one doesn't know what the other one is doing with their money. So, what's the solution? How do you obtain financial intimacy?

Here's What Worked for Me ...

My wife and I have multiple bank accounts that allow us to maintain financial transparency in our marriage, and at the same time provide financial stability and independence for each other.

All income initially gets deposited into our joint account. A set amount ("allocation") is then deposited by the bank into each of the individual accounts each pay period.

Example of our Bank Accounts:

Account #1–Individual – Separate checking account
Account #2–Individual – Separate checking account
Account #3–Joint household account–bills on auto pay
Account #4–MMA Savings (money market account/ savings account)–MMA usually gives more interest than regular savings accounts–look that up → Designate a certain amount to be automatically transferred to savings each month (this should be a sufficient amount to achieve the financial goal you have set for the year for savings)
Account #5-Investments - Property, stocks, mutual funds, bonds, silent partner, Roth IRA → joint account
Account #6–Vacations, entertainment, eating out → joint account (optional)

Tips to Make it Work:

All funds from all paychecks and income get deposited into the joint accounts.

—Funds spent from the individual accounts are just that - individual. Each person is allotted a certain amount on a bi-weekly or monthly basis to cover his/her individual expenses. Don't go crazy here. If you only need $1,500 a month, that's all you should get. Remember, we're changing mindsets and living a life that makes sense financially. Focus on things that make sense to maintain yourself monthly, i.e., personal care, hair, nails, lunch, gas expenses, auxiliary organizations, etc.

— Place notifications on the joint account–a notification is sent to each party automatically from the bank if an expenditure is made over $200.

— All bills should be paid from the joint account on autopay.

— Discuss any expenditure over $500 before you spend the funds to make sure both parties are comfortable.

— Discuss lending money to others, including family...especially family.

— Both parties should have equal access to accounts #3-6.

8. BE THE 5%

In any organization, you have those who do what they're supposed to do, those who try to manipulate the system, and then you have the 5%.

85% of people come to work, do what they're supposed to do, and go home (same in most families).

10% of people cause 90% of the problems. Supervisors often spend 90% of their time dealing with 10% of the people. I call them knuckleheads.

5% of people are those I call the "5-percenters." These are the people who will get it done. These are your subject -matter experts, people who come to work on time, go the extra mile, and if you ask them to do something, you know they will get it done. It's hard to fire a 5-percenter or not give them a raise. If you're a 5-percenter, and you want to work, it's highly unlikely that you will be without a job.

I am a 5-percenter. My wife is a 5-percenter. When there is a difficult task to do, we are the people that others call to get it done. Before I retired, I prided myself on being a 5-percenter. If you are that person, your employer will notice, and your family and friends will notice. Be a freaking 5-percenter!

9. TYPES OF INVESTORS

There are four main types of investors: (i) non-investor; (ii) passive investor; (iii) active investor; and (iv) accredited investor.

Non-investor - Person who doesn't generally invest. This person is more comfortable with an "enjoy life now" mindset instead of looking down the road. This person generally deals with things as they come. Their mindset is "I can't take it with me, so I'm going to spend it now."

Passive investor - Most of us are in this category. You might have a 401k, IRA, general savings, or stock, but not much more. These are great starter investments, but I encourage clients to participate in other types of investments because these investments almost exclusively rely on someone else for success.

When the housing market crashed, a lot of 401ks went with it. Under a 401k plan, an employer may match what you invest. If you invest 1%, your employer may match your contribution dollar for dollar. If you put more money in, your employer may increase its contribution as well. If your employer will match up to 6% under the plan, then you should invest up to 6% to get the maximum match possible from your employer. Don't leave that money on the table because this could turn out to be a large number over time.

Active investor - This is a person who looks at the market and tries to find ways to make money.

Example - Warren Buffet. He and his buddies came up with a system to look at the volatility of stock, capitalized on it, and became rich. My retirement pay comes from the military, but I don't trust the government to sustain that pay so I looked for an avenue that would allow me to invest in something stable. I chose real estate.

I track the market to make sure my investment remains a good investment. Take advantage of circumstances as much as possible and use the money you invest to find other ways to make money.

Accredited Investor – According to www.seekingalpha. com, a leading stock market website, an accredited investor is one who meets certain Securities Exchange Commission (SEC) requirements, including minimum levels of income, investment experience, and net worth to qualify for investing in more restrictive investment opportunities.

Example - If a government authority wants to build a toll road, the authority can seek a group of private investors and use private funds to build the road. That road will be there for many years to come. Accredited investors get the money from the tolls for life. However, in order to invest, you have to first meet the requirements to be an accredited investor and prove that you will continue to meet the criteria in the future.

What I Want from You:

Initially, I want you to be a passive investor. Once you become comfortable with that, I challenge you to transition to being an active investor. Do the research on how to exercise control and capitalize when an opportunity presents itself. Now that you have read this section, think about what kind of investor you want to be. Continue to be a life-long learner and invest your money in things that will make you more money.

10. IGNORING THE INEVITABLE PROBLEM

As mentioned in a previous section, the "ostrich effect" is a financial bias that lends itself to the false narrative that ostriches hide their heads in the sand to ignore danger or pretend that it does not exist as a way of protecting themselves.[22] People do the same with things that threaten to cause financial dangers. How many times have you heard a noise from your car or looked at something in your house that needed to be repaired, and you just ignored it? Later, you ended up paying so much more than you would have if you had just dealt with the issue immediately.

---

22. "The Ostrich Effect: When We Hide From Our Finances," Santander, January 17, 2022. https://www.santander.com/en/stories/the-ostrich-effect-when-we-hide-from-our-finances#:~:text=What%20lies%20behind%20a%20bad,how%20we%20can%20fight%20it.

11. COMMUNICATION IS KEY

Communication is the key to any successful relationship. You have to communicate properly, interpret effectively, and take action. One of the most important aspects of communication is the ability to listen. Good communicators listen for understanding, not just to respond. In the Army, we did a "brief back" to confirm understanding of what the person was trying to communicate. If someone communicates with you, your response would be, "Okay, what I hear you saying is... ." It is imperative that you communicate to build relationships with your spouse, partner, family, co-workers, and friends.

12. CHAMPAGNE TASTE/KOOL-AID MONEY

When I first joined the Army, I had champagne taste and Kool-Aid money. I wanted the best clothes, cars, food, apartment, etc., but I couldn't afford the best on my income. This is where being frugal comes into play. I had to learn to find a way to achieve the best quality items without spending beyond my means or paying a higher price for something that didn't have the value for the asking price.

I love suits and I love looking good. I often go to the thrift store and buy a suit for $35, then take it to the tailor for a custom fit for $50. That gives me a tailor-made suit for less than $100. I don't buy new cars. I usually buy cars that are two to four years old to allow depreciation. A new car loses value as soon as you drive it off the car lot. If you finance a new car and get into an accident and total the car, you will likely owe more on the car than it's worth. This is commonly called being "upside down" on a vehicle loan. If you wait at least two years, the car will have depreciated in value and you will probably pay closer to what it's actually worth.

I rarely pay retail price for anything. Time decreases value on most things. If you exercise patience and wait just a little while, prices will generally go down.

13. NETWORKING WORKS

You must network. It's not about who you know; it's about who knows you! The more people that know you, the more you will be considered for that promotion or position you've been trying to get. When people can speak your name when you're not in the room, you've done a good job of networking. Networking has gotten many people their jobs. If you're not on LinkedIn, get on it. If your LinkedIn account is outdated, update it. If all you do is go to work and go home, that's all you will get.

Networking can also provide you with the invaluable experience of having a mentor. If you want to be good at something, the best thing you can do is find someone in that industry that you consider successful and learn from them.

One of the best people I met in real estate when I first started was Juan Garcia. From 1993-1994, when I was stationed in Korea, I started doing extensive research and listening to a real estate course by renowned real estate investor and best-selling author Carleton Sheets. After I came back to the US, I started putting that knowledge to work. I was stationed at Sheppard Air Force Base in Wichita Falls, Texas, in 1997. That is when I bought my first property, and where I met Juan.

At Sheppard, I was an instructor for the dental apprentice course for three branches of the military. Juan operated the computer-based testing facility where my students took their tests. At the beginning of my class, I would ask my students an ice breaker question, which was, "Can you tell me something about yourself that most people don't know?" One day, I was waiting for my students to complete their test and Juan and I stepped outside to chat. I decided to ask Juan my ice breaker question, and I was surprised by his response. He said, "A lot of people don't know that I own 50 properties." This really surprised me, and I was excited to tell him I had been studying to become an investor. That was our connection.

Juan took me under his wing and I learned so much from him. He taught me so much about the business that probably would have taken me years, and many mistakes, to learn on my own. I increased my real estate investing knowledge by leaps and bounds through his mentorship. I will forever be thankful to him.

Other great networking tips:

- Join professional organizations in the industry you're pursuing;
- Subscribe to industry magazines, e-newsletters, email lists, or follow on social media;
- Listen to podcasts; and
- Attend industry conferences.

14. STAY READY

Being ready counts. I need you to be prepared.

My aunt Debra was one of my favorite people in the world. One day, she asked me what I wanted to be when I got older? I told her I wanted to be like the 'fly jock' Tom Joyner!

My aunt always told me, "If you want to do something, don't just talk about it, be about it. Go out there and make it happen."

In order to achieve your dreams, you have to be ready when the opportunity comes along. When I was stationed at Fort Stewart, Georgia, in 1995, I applied to be a radio personality at WSKX radio. I had no experience but dropped off my application anyway. The station manager said, "Don't call us, we'll call you." Needless to say, I didn't expect to hear from her. But to my surprise, about two months later, the radio station called and asked me to come in for an interview. I was so excited!

I went down to the station and quickly realized this was not a regular interview. This was for an on-air personality. I get in the room, the light comes on in five seconds, and when the light comes on, she said, "Read this statement." I read the statement and the producer said, "I thought you didn't have any experience?"

I said, "I don't, but I've been practicing for years to be a radio personality, and my Aunt Debra told me to always be ready!"

She was so impressed that she gave me an internship for three weeks. After the three weeks, she gave me a Saturday position on the radio at WSKX. I talked to tens of thousands of people every weekend for almost two years, and it was great. It was one of the best experiences of my life, but what I learned was that I really didn't want to live the life of a radio personality. The moral of the story is I got the position because I was ready.

What I'm asking from you is to be ready for financial opportunities when they present themselves. Think about the first day of school in anatomy and physiology class. Imagine the advantage you would have on the first day, if you knew all the bones in the body.

Being prepared will make you that 5-percenter.

15. WHAT DOES SUCCESS LOOK LIKE TO YOU?

Generally, we define success with money, fancy cars, designer clothes, big houses, or materialistic things. Those things do provide a certain status in life, but I encourage you to look at success based on these things as well:

— Your physical health;

— Mental health;

— Having free time; and

— Doing what you love.

Free time is worth more than six figures. I retired at the age of 44. I have found that the ability to get up every day and do exactly what I want to do, when I want to do it, is priceless.

Having money allows you to do things that you love to do, not just the things you have to do.

What is your definition of success? _____

_____

_____

_____

Who do you know personally that you consider
successful? _____

_____

_____

_____

16. BEING RESPONSIBLE PAYS

Being a responsible person yields a return on your
investment. It saves you money, and it makes you money.
I'm challenging you to be successful from this point
forward. You know what it takes to be the responsible
person on your job, in your family, in your organizations
… do what you're supposed to do!

17. HOW HARD DO YOU WORK FOR SOMEONE
ELSE?

We work hard for other people, and that's okay because
we do what we have to do to survive. I want you to be a
5-percenter, but imagine if you worked just as hard for
yourself as you do for someone else. It's important to find
the time to work on you and your goals, even if you work
a full-time job. Most people with full-time jobs spend at
least 40 hours a week making someone else rich. Use that
same energy to find time to work *on* yourself *for* yourself.

Two things I wanted to do in life were to be a radio personality and a stand-up comedian. I was a Staff Sergeant in the Army, raising my pre-teen daughter as a single parent, and in class two days a week working on my Bachelor's degree. Yet, I found time to work on things I wanted to do to be successful. I focused on my radio personality gig, and practiced my stand-up comedy routine to be ready when an opportunity presented itself. I was able to achieve both. If you put in the time and work as hard on your goals as you do on someone else's, you will have a greater chance of achieving your goals and dreams. Invest in YOU!

18. CHOOSE YOUR LIFE PARTNER WISELY

One of the most important decisions you make in your life is choosing the person to spend it with! Think about the decision-making process of considering a new job. Generally you assess salary, industry, location, upward opportunities, etc. Take that same approach when assessing your life partner. What are your preferences? Make a list of the qualities that you prefer in a partner. Place an asterisk by the things that are non-negotiables.

Example - My list included about 20 things. If I had an asterisk by "no smoking," and I met a woman that smokes, I wouldn't go out with her. Why would I? That's a deal breaker. It would be a waste of my time and hers because I knew I could never be in a serious relationship with a woman who smokes.

Use the list to provide guidance throughout the relationship. When you're dating, if something comes up that is a non-negotiable, then it's time to consider ending the relationship. People are who they are, but you shouldn't accept something while you're dating someone and then expect it to change after you get married.

Know what you want, make your list, and stick to it. However, don't be so unrealistic in making your list that you miss out on a great partner. Never try to change someone into what you want. Accept them for who they are.

Most importantly, you can't be a nickel looking for a dime. Read that again.

19. FRUGAL VS. CHEAP

There is a big difference between being frugal vs. being cheap. Frugal people usually only buy things that have value, whereas cheap people try to get things for free.

Example – I buy off-brand items at the grocery store all the time. I created a "frugal vs. cheap" challenge for some of my family members.

I issued the challenge that if we did a side-by-side comparison, they wouldn't be able to tell the difference between the name brand vs. the off-brand. I blindfolded four of my family members and placed these items below in front of them:

Oreo cookies/Great Value twist and shouts
Reynolds Wrap/Great Value aluminum foil
Jif peanut butter/Great Value peanut butter
Premium crackers/Great Value crackers

None of my family members correctly identified all four of the name brands. This challenge showed that frugal products can be as good as name brand and they cost less. Please note, this doesn't work for all off-brand items.

Tips to Make it Work:

If you use coupons, only buy what you need. Don't just buy something because you have a coupon.

Loaning money to your family - My rationale for loaning money to family members is that I will give you a "hand-up," but not a "hand-out."

Example - Previously, I discussed the scenario if a family member wanted to buy a car that cost $4,000 and she had $3,200 and asked to borrow $800, I would probably loan her the $800. I consider that a "hand-up" to helping her better her life as opposed to a handout. However, if she had $800, and asked me to loan her $3,200, I would not loan her the money. I would have more skin in the game than her. I call that a "hand out."

Be able to say no to your family members for hand-outs. When you give a hand-up, don't loan what you can't afford to lose because you may not get it back. You need to be okay with that. Note: If you don't get your money back, take that person off of your loan list - permanently.

20. MAKING PERMANENT DECISIONS BASED ON TEMPORARY FEELINGS

Avoid making long-term decisions when you're angry, frustrated, mad, or sad. We've all probably done this and regretted it later.

Example - You change your major in college because you're frustrated with one class, then later realize you hate your new major. You join the military just to get out of your parents' house and later realize the military is not for you. You move in with someone you've only dated for a few weeks because you're so in love and then realize they're a slob and you can't live together.

How do you avoid this? If you're in a room full of smoke, the door could be five feet in front of you, but you can't see because of the smoke. If you give it a few minutes, the smoke will clear, and you will be able to see your way out. Similarly, if you're highly emotional or upset, give yourself a minute, an hour, a day, or maybe even a week to calm down and let the smoke clear before you make a drastic decision that will permanently affect your life.

21. EATING OUT

The average person who works outside the home spends $15 for lunch. If you eat out for lunch five days a week, that's $75 a week and $300 a month on lunch. If you eat out regularly during the week for dinner, that's an additional monthly expense for food. This is not sustainable for most people's budget. Meal prepping and taking your lunch to work will prevent youfrom overspending.

For example, I can make seven meals for about $10:
Rotisserie chicken from Sam's Club = $5
1 pound bag of rice = $1.25
Broccoli florets = $3.50 (yields seven servings)

These numbers may not be exact, but my point is that taking your lunch to work and meal prepping are two of the most efficient and economical ways to avoid overspending on meals. Eating out for lunch burns a lot of your disposable income, in turn making it harder to sustain a healthy budget.

22. GETTING OUT OF YOUR COMFORT ZONE

At some point in your life, you have to be uncomfortable to succeed. Ask yourself right now, are you uncomfortable in your life? Are you doing anything extra besides going to work and coming home? If you're sitting at home, every night, not doing anything different, you're probably not uncomfortable.

In order to advance, you have to be uncomfortable. Anything you do that leads to success is likely going to make you uncomfortable. Getting in shape, saving money, getting an advanced degree, all of these things push you out of your comfort zone.

These things can cause sleepless nights, early mornings, and anxious moments, but succeeding in these areas of your life means that you're excelling and moving forward. Don't just stand still in your life. You have to sacrifice to achieve your goals.

Stop right now and look back at your life plan. What are your plans to advance your education or your career? Are you doing those things? If not, I challenge you right now to step outside of your box and push yourself to achieve your goals and dreams. Nothing worth having is easy.

23. CRAWL, WALK, RUN

This concept is based on the evolution of human life. We each have five phases in our lives. Let's break down the first three phases.

(i) *Crawl Phase* - The early years when you're learning about the basics of life (hot/cold, yes/no, right/wrong, etc).

(ii) *Walk Phase* - Teenage into early adulthood – learning about love, failure, disappointment, starting to know your wants and desires, developing your personality, morals and ethics, understanding who to trust or not trust.

(iii) *Run Phase* - This phase is often referred to as the "prime of your life." This is the strongest you will be with the highest mental agility and the time when you will move the fastest. You should have attained your advanced degree by this time. Don't walk or crawl in the run phase – you are in your 20s, 30s, 40s and early 50s. This is the money-making phase of your life. You should be learning, developing, acquiring wealth and assets, capitalizing on your education, and taking advantage of opportunities for promotions and advancement as much as possible. Your goals in this phase are to advance, challenge yourself and make money - you need to be running…even if you have to pivot and change course to do it!

Example - I didn't start my career path to becoming an officer in the Army until I was 33. Most people start that journey in their early 20s. Because I started late, I knew early on that I would never be a full bird Colonel, or even a Lieutenant Colonel because of the time and effort it would require to achieve that level. I was not willing to commit to obtain the highest level of promotion; however, I knew the change I was making at 33 would help me improve my status in the military and achieve my goal of becoming an officer. The end game was to retire at a higher salary and rank, so I knew I would have to pivot during my run phase.

Now, let's look at the last two phases.

(iv) *Walk Phase* - Late 50s and 60s - These are generally the early retirement years, but if you're not retired, you're most likely settled into your career and not looking to start a new one. Most people in this phase of life usually are not looking to obtain an advanced degree; however, you may have those one-offs who have "always wanted to obtain a PhD" so they begin to pursue another career later in life, but that's the exception not the rule.

(v) *Crawl Phase* – 70s and beyond – These are well into your retirement years, and you should be living off of your assets. This is the time when you're passing down your legacy and preparing to enter the next journey. What you don't want to do is be in the crawl phase of your life and realize that you didn't do enough during the run phase, to sustain yourself during the crawl phase. If you don't understand that, read it again.

24. INVEST IN YOUR COMMUNITY

You've probably heard the phrase, "To whom much is given, much is required." It's important to me to give back to the community and make an impact beyond the cultural norm. My wife and I are both lifetime community volunteers, mentors, and we firmly believe in educating the youth to sustain the future. We started the McGinnis Legacy Foundation to provide annual scholarships for high school students to attend college, train future leaders, and educate the masses on financial literacy.

Annually, the McGinnis Legacy Foundation partners with the Arlington Grand-Prairie Guide Right Foundation[23] to award the *Debra Mary Barnes Scholarship* to the beau with the highest GPA who also participates in the annual beautillion. The McGinnis Legacy Foundation also partners with the Arlington Foundation for Excellence in Education[24] to award the *Mel Brown McGinnis Legacy Arts Scholarship* to a college-bound high school senior who wants to pursue a career in literary, visual, or performing arts.

Additionally, my wife and I provide financial support for various non-profit organizations. This allows us to support our community and provides a benefit on our tax returns. If you are blessed with an education and a successful career, I encourage you to invest in your community with your time, energy, and financial resources. Find something that really matters to you and support that cause. Donations to non-profit organizations can generally be deducted and can reduce your tax liability when you file taxes.**

** Note: If you plan to donate to a charity or non-profit organization, visit with your tax professional to ensure your contribution is tax-deductible.

---

23. The Arlington Grand-Prairie Guide Right Foundation is the 501(c)(3) fundraising arm of the Arlington Grand-Prairie Alumni Chapter of Kappa Alpha Psi Fraternity, Inc., - www.agpgrf.com.

24. The Arlington Foundation for Excellence in Education is the 501(c)(3) partner of the Xi Theta Omega Chapter of Alpha Kappa Alpha Sorority, Inc., www.arlingtoneducation.org.

25. INVEST IN YOURSELF

The very last thing I want to impart upon you is the importance of investing in yourself. It's important that you invest in yourself professionally to advance your career or your position in your chosen industry. Often times we hesitate to spend the money to advance our careers. It's great to have your employer pay for those additional courses, but if you're the employer as an entrepreneur, that may not be an option available to you. You have to be willing to spend the money yourself.

Don't be afraid to invest in yourself so that you can climb the ladder in your profession, whatever it may be. Having that additional degree or certification can set you apart from your peers and give you the advantage in getting that promotion. Having a professional certification shows initiative and that you're willing to hone your craft and become an expert in your field.

Using myself as an example, my thirst for knowledge never ends. I have a master's degree, a bachelor's degree, and five associates degrees. Beyond college, I received certifications in the dental and financial industries. I continuously seek professional development and educational opportunities that give me an edge in my professional arena. I want you to do the same.

I'm not asking you to take some get-rich-quick course that promises to "make you a million dollars in six months." That usually doesn't come to fruition. I'm asking you to identify opportunities that will help you advance your career and take those extra courses to obtain industry certifications. Professional development courses often give you a great return on your investment and go a long way in advancing your career. Spend the money and invest in YOU.

CONGRATULATIONS!

If you've reached the end of this book, then you know the concept is not about trying to game the system, nor is it about trying to shun responsibility; it's about digging deep, working hard, being disciplined, and making things happen. I wrote this book because I'm frustrated with people trying to hack the system, avoid responsibility, and spend so much time trying to avoid proper money management. If you reached the end of this book, you know the path of least resistance is not the way to go. Don't try to pass off the hard work. You will spend more time trying to avoid the necessary things you have to do to be successful, than being successful.

Here's what I want you to takeaway:

This book is about being responsible with your life and your money, being mature, and working smarter not harder. Doing the things I've asked you to do in this book are not easy. But these are proven techniques that will help you achieve your financial goals. Dig in, get your mind right, and make it happen!

Always remember…

Mindset First Money Second.

JBMcGinn

FINANCIAL LITERACY EXPERT

NOTES:

www.jbmseminars.com

Made in the USA
Columbia, SC
08 October 2024

43945622R10076